Psalms
for all seasons

Also by David Allan Hubbard

WITH BANDS OF LOVE:
Lessons from the Book of Hosea

Psalms
for all seasons

by

DAVID ALLAN HUBBARD

William B. Eerdmans Publishing Company
Grand Rapids, Michigan

The chapters in this book were offered as a series of talks on the international radio broadcast "The Joyful Sound." Credit for the final editing goes to my brother Robert L. Hubbard, Sr., and to Cliff Pederson, Director of Publications for the Gospel Broadcasting Association.

Contents

Introduction

Open your Bible in the middle and what do you find? The Book of Psalms, of course. There's something symbolic about this because for centuries the Psalms have been in the center, in the heart of the worship of God's people.

In the Jerusalem Temple for nearly a thousand years, from the time of Solomon until the Roman invasion under Titus, the Jews lifted their voices in praise or lamentation through the Psalms. Who can doubt that the Psalms were used by Paul and Silas during their midnight songfest in the Philippian jail? And the walls of European monasteries echoed throughout the middle ages with the chanting of the Psalms.

The Reformers planted the Psalter in the heart of their services. In Scotland and Holland the Psalms became the chief expression of the believers' newly recovered faith in the God of the Bible. When the singing of praise, previously reserved to priests and monks, once again became the privilege of God's whole priestly people, the Psalms were the way they chose.

It's no accident that the Psalms have had this magnetic effect in drawing the people of God to live within their pages. The Psalms are unrivaled in their range and power of expression. From praise to lament, from petition to complaint, from celebrating

7

God's grace to begging him for more help, from assurance to anxiety, from the vowing of thanksgiving to the voicing of disappointment, all the emotions and responses of the human spirit are expressed. Devoutly, honestly, beautifully, forcefully, the feelings of the believing heart come through.

This does not mean that the Psalms are more important than the Gospels or Epistles, which speak to us of God's special grace through Jesus Christ. No, apart from the life, death and resurrection of Christ we would have no Christian Bible at all.

But I do mean that the Psalms were central even to Christ's devotion and worship. Christ's words were so salted with quotations from the Psalms that he must have committed them to memory. Nailed upon the cross, cursed for man's sin, Christ poured out his anguish in words from the opening lines of Psalm 22: "My God, my God, why hast thou forsaken me?"

No wonder the first Christians worshipped God with "psalms and hymns and spiritual songs" (Colossians 3:16). This was most natural. After all, this was the way their Master worshipped. Christ's example and the disciples' experience have combined to set a tradition for the Christian church which shall never cease.

You too can receive the blessings of this great tradition. Begin now to read the Psalms. Your private devotion and public worship will become more meaningful as you read the words which God's servants speak to God. The human interest stories will carry you on from page to page. Every phase of life is pictured: joys, sorrows, victories, defeats, wearying struggles, shameful disgraces, monotonous ploddings, and exuberant glories. That's why we can call the Psalms, "Psalms for All Seasons."

CHAPTER 1

Stability in Undisciplined Days

PSALM 1

A formula for happiness, that's what the first psalm is all about, a formula that works even in undisciplined days. There are lots of formulas being fed into the computers of life today. The one thing we don't lack is advice. "Do your own thing." "Enjoy yourself." Or on the other hand, there are those who urge us to join their group, to pledge ourselves to keep their rules, to follow their formulas, to let them make our decisions for us.

In a world of lawlessness and licence, a great temptation for sensitive people is to combat looseness with legalism. Psalm 1 is a great help to us just at this point. It reminds us of the importance of God's law, God's instructions, without leading us into the trap of legalism—legalism which is a basic opponent, a relentless foe of the gospel of Jesus Christ. Psalm 1 is a psalm for all seasons, but particularly for undisciplined days.

We don't need to squander any time documenting the lack of discipline today. The riots in our cities, the violent protests on our campuses, the rampaging crime rate, the political unrest—these are all symptoms of our lack of discipline.

How does a concerned Christian react? That's a good question. And our greatest danger is overreacting. We cannot be complacent, true. But to over-react into rigidity is just as bad. It seems to me that the answer to undisciplined days is **better disciple-ship.** That's what will give us stability.

Discipleship takes its orders and forms its patterns in obedience to the will of God, not merely in re-sponse to the tone of society. We are not to let the world squeeze us into its mold, nor are we to let it force us into some non-Christian attitude in our attempt to escape worldliness.

1. Concern for Sinners versus Companionship with Them

And so the first thing we want to see from Psalm 1 is **the difference between our concern for sinners and our companionship with them.** This psalm, like the whole Bible, is realistic about sin. It reckons with its seriousness and measures its attractiveness. Like the wisdom to be found in Proverbs, the advice here centers first in avoiding open flagrant sin. And how we need this kind of advice! We are so surrounded by the ravages of sin that we come to accept it as a way of life. We read about it in magazines and newspapers, and we see it in the cinema and on television. We hear about it in the coffee breaks where we work, and we know its power in our own drives and desires.

The psalmist uses a pattern of repetition to show just how sin lures and traps those who play around with it. The progressive steps in the description of sin are obvious. "Happy is the man," the psalmist says, "who does not walk, stand, or sit in the ways of sinners" (v. 1). Note how the verbs picture the stages in which sin ensnares us. We may **walk** casually into an act of sin; but that act, if not checked, can become a habit in which we **stand;** and finally that habit can develop into a way of life in which we **sit,** entrenched, immobilized, helpless.

The same progression is seen in the nouns which describe the wicked people whose patterns attract us. The **wicked** or the ungodly in the psalm is the man who gives way to temptation from time to time. The **sinner** is the deep-grained breaker of God's will. The **scoffer** is not only wicked himself but scorns and jeers at anybody who tries to do right. Flirt with sin, and you'll become enslaved. That's the warning of this psalm.

At the same time we remember that our Lord spent time with just the kind of people this psalm describes. Our task then is not to avoid them or to shun them, if we are to be true disciples, but to seek to share our faith and life with them. We can be concerned for them; we can demonstrate our care without cutting ourselves off from them. We are forbidden to follow their advice, that is, to walk in their counsel. We are forbidden to emulate their habits, that is, to stand in their way. We are forbidden to immerse ourselves in their form of life, that is, to sit in their seat. Concern for them, and commitment to them without compromise—that's what discipleship is all about. So we see the difference between concern for sinners and the wrong kind of companionship with them.

2. Love of Law versus Legalism

The second difference we want to see through this psalm is **the difference between love of law and legalism.** It's one thing to delight in the law; it's another to depend upon it.

We want to see the background of the law in order to understand the importance of the law. The law was given as an act of grace after the exodus—not as a means of gaining God's favor, but as a way of responding to the grace that God had already shown. It was God's loving act of letting his people know his will.

The Hebrew word used for "law" (Torah) in the psalm means the full instruction of God, especially the instructions contained in the first five books of the Bible called the Pentateuch. For the Jews the law not only meant what they were to do, but more important, what God had done for them. The best defense against temptation is not the reminder of what we ought to do but the memory of what God has done for us. This attitude toward law is a useful antidote against legalism.

We also want to see the divine origin of the law in contrast with human traditions which are so often harsh and contrary and against which we are so apt to rebel. And we ought to see the divine origin of the law in contrast with pagan superstition, those dark areas of taboo, of sacred spell and of mumbo-jumbo magic.

Man has tried to build his own Sinais by making mountains out of the molehills of his own standards or his own religious practices. But I want you to know that legalism is a curse because it implies that we can please God by something we do. Legalism is insolence; delighting in the law is discipleship.

No wonder the psalmist could delight in the law and urge us to delve into its delights with him. At the heart of the law is the call to love—to love God and man. No wonder James could call it a perfect law, a law of liberty, a royal law (1:25; 2:8, 12).

Did you note the contrast between the love of law and lawlessness in the results that have been described? The man who loves the law is stable; he's planted like a tree. He's refreshed; he lives by streams of water (v. 3). Think what that means in a dry, desert context. He's fruitful; he brings forth the fruit of good character at the right time. Love and joy and peace are working in his life. There's continuity: he's constant and steadfast; his leaf does not wither; and there's prosperity in all that he does.

Now look at the other side of the story—the wicked. They're unstable; they lack fruit. They're like chaff (v. 4). That is, they're lifeless; they carry no weight. You know that chaff is a nuisance to the farmer or the thresher. He has to get rid of it. He has to beat the grain in such a way that the chaff rises into the air and is carried away with the wind so that he can get at the real grain from which to grind his meal.

And the wicked person cannot pass the test of God's judgment (v. 5). The mention of judgment reminds us that there is in the Bible a doctrine of the two ways. The New Testament picks this up as well.

In our modern day we're apt to talk about shades of gray. And yet even in the midst of the twentieth century there are blacks and whites, aren't there? When you go to the hospital, there's a lot of difference between life and death. When you're in court there's a world of difference between being guilty and not being guilty. In many areas there are two ways and certainly in the area of the spiritual life.

Christ mentioned the broad way and the narrow way, the corrupt tree and the good tree, the house built on sand and the one founded on the rock (Matthew 7:13-14, 17, 24-27). And the psalmist talks about the way of those who walk in sin and the way of those who delight in God's will. One way peters out and perishes; and the other way is loved and known and cherished by God (v. 6). Everyone, everyone I say, walks one of these two ways. Which way are you walking?

Prayer: Thank you, Father, for not leaving us on our own to try to figure out what is right. Thank you especially for Jesus Christ who is the way, the truth and the life. In His Name we pray. Amen.

CHAPTER 2

The Last Laugh

PSALM 2

"There are two things we should never discuss: religion and politics." This common bit of advice may help to keep things peaceful at a party, but it can scarcely stand careful scrutiny anywhere else. If avoiding arguments is our main aim in life, then we will do well to skirt questions of religious belief or political conviction. But certainly there are higher goals to be reached than merely shunning controversy.

The biblical psalmists were not at all embarrassed to talk about both religion and politics, and they often did so in the same psalm. We are tempted, in our Western European way, to fence life into categories, into separate plots of thought and action that barely touch each other. But not the men of Israel. They knew that their God, the one true and living God, was Lord of all of life. And among their company were psalmists like the author of the second psalm.

Far from avoiding the tension between religion and politics, this biblical writer affirms that our religious faith affects every other area of living. The attitude of many of us toward religion is symbolized by the format followed in news magazines like **Time** or **Newsweek.** Here religion is a subject to be surveyed with other subjects like sports, business, law, medicine, movies and books. But for the person who really knows what faith is all about, this type of compartmentalization will not do. Our religious faith ultimately governs every aspect of our living. Anyone who thinks that his religion is a subject that he can keep to himself has not yet been gripped by the message of the Bible.

If we are committed to a biblical view of life, we can neither be silent about religion and politics nor can we treat them as separate realms. The reason is clear: politics has a deep, religious purpose; and religion has profound political implications.

Before we see how Psalm 2 substantiates this statement, we should make clear what we mean by **politics**. Obviously, I am not pushing for a particular candidate or party. Nor am I saying that all Christians should vote alike. What I do mean, however, is that we must be vitally interested in how we are governed—and not only in how **we** are governed but how **other people** are governed. And we do this not only for the sake of the people being governed but for the sake of the government itself.

If this seems a bit complicated, stick with me while we see what the psalmist has to say. His words about the relationship between divine and human governments are always in season and never more so than in this day of revolution and counterrevolution, of international power plays and domestic political confusion.

1. The Nations Are Limited in Power

Psalm 2 begins with a news bulletin announcing a revolutionary international conspiracy. A coalition of kings is plotting to declare their independence from the king of Israel, whom God has enabled to subdue and control them (vv. 1-4). Just who these nations were and when they took counsel against the Lord and his anointed king we do not know. Most likely they were the kingdoms of Ammon, Moab, and Edom located to the east and south of Jerusalem. Both David and Solomon had dominated those regions, and from time to time succeeding kings of Judah had done likewise.

More important than the identity of the conspiring nations is the optimism of the psalmist. No panic seizes his soul as he hears the news. The plot neither pressures him to act in frenzy nor paralyzes him into immobility. He knows something we all must learn: nations are limited in power.

They are limited in power because their authority is restricted to earth. Their rulers and their people—no matter how influential or how affluent—are still human regardless of their vaunted pomp and show. This limitation is dramatized in the contrast which the psalmist draws: the kings of the **earth** are no match for the Lord that sits in the **heavens** (v. 4).

It is in heaven that the ultimate authority lies. This is why God can laugh while kings rage. Their rule is dependent on God's authority, not his on theirs. As the apostle Paul analyzes it, "There is no authority except from God, and those that exist have been instituted by God" (Romans 13:1).

Kings are not only human (though in the ancient orient they often claimed to be divine), but their very right to rule is derived from God and is dependent on his authority. Their governments have one main purpose: to exercise justice among the people or, as Peter summarized it, "to punish those who do wrong and to praise those who do right" (I Peter 2:14).

2. The Nations May Become Hostile in Intent

Sin takes its toll on nations as well as individuals. Political leaders can make grave mistakes like anyone else. They may misread their God-given purpose and then mislead the people under their authority.

Governments exercise substantial power. They raise taxes, maintain armies, regulate commerce, engage in huge financial transactions. Through concentrated political effort they can solve difficult problems. Cities are redeveloped, frontier lands are civilized, technological breakthroughs are made, crime is kept in check. But this power to deal with problems is deceptive, even seductive.

Governments can readily gain the idea that they can make their own laws and pursue any policy that pleases them without regard for God. They may chafe against the limitations God has imposed on them. They may, without really knowing it, resent his absolute authority and try to wrest it from him.

A dictatorship or totalitarian state does this. It takes all authority to itself as though it, not God, were the highest authority. It may rigidly regulate every area of life including worship. When it does, it plays god for the very people it should serve. And, of course, when anyone or anything but God tries to be God, the results are diabolical—diabolical because the devil's oldest ploy is to lure us into thinking that we are or can be divine.

When nations ambitiously, ruthlessly set out to snatch for themselves territory that belongs to others, they are guilty of a kind of blasphemy. It is God who governs the course of history and ultimately determines the boundaries of the kingdoms of the world. Selfish expansion and the cruel conflict that often goes with it are attempts to seize the helm of history from God's hand—an insolent act if there ever was one!

Nations are limited in their power, and, because they are, they may harbor hostile intentions. They may go so far as to turn on the God from whom their authority is derived. They may reject their divinely appointed function, which is to reflect in earthly contexts the concern for justice that is characteristic of God's kingdom. Ambition and oppression may become their style of life. And when this happens, they stand under God's judgment, because it is he who grants the charter for their existence.

3. The Nations Are Subject to God's Sovereignty

No note is sounded more strongly in the second psalm than God's full sovereignty. While kings plot on earth, God sits in heaven. While nations rage in rebellion, God laughs in derision. Not at all fazed by their bitter conspiracy, he sits unthreatened, secure in the knowledge of his own power and glory.

To his appointed king God has delegated his rule, and through him he will cool the nations' boiling ambition. So close is the relationship between God and the king of Judah that he calls the ruler his adopted son: "You are my son, today I have begotten you" (v. 7). The idea is not that the king was divine but that he stood in a special relationship to God, that he was committed to serving God and carrying out his will.

Few kings in Israel's history truly fulfilled this expectation. David, Solomon, Asa, Jehoshaphat, Hezekiah, and Josiah just about complete the list. But in the four centuries of history spanned by their reigns there were far more examples of sorry than shining kings. By and large the kings of Judah and Israel were as ambitious and oppressive, insolent and brutal as their Gentile counterparts.

The very failure of Israel's kings to serve God was used by him to pave the way for the coming of the true king who was to shoulder the government of the world in the name of God. A psalm like this can be called Messianic because in a wonderfully accurate and compelling way it points to the coming of Christ, whose kingdom shall know no end.

Ultimately, the kingdoms of the earth have to reckon with Christ. For the time is coming when "the kingdom of the world has become the kingdom of our Lord and of his Christ, and he shall reign for ever and ever" (Revelation 11:15). Just to hear these words in a day of political turmoil and international strife makes us want to break out in a resounding "Hallelujah Chorus."

But our political rulers don't have to wait until then to accept Christ's rule, any more than the rest of us do. The invitation of our psalmist still holds: "Now therefore, O kings, be wise; be warned, O rulers of the earth. Serve the Lord with fear" (vv. 10, 11).

God's last word to them and to us is not a laugh of derision at our arrogant independence. It is an invitation to take refuge in him, a refuge in which even the mightiest nations need to trust if they are to be truly secure.

Prayer: Great God, our heavenly king, in a day when many despise their governments bitterly and others depend upon them naively, grant us clear per-

spective. Help us to see that you are ruler over all and that our basic allegiance must be to you. Teach us to be responsible citizens who know both the function of governments and their limitations. Above all, teach us to crown Jesus Christ, your Son, as king of our lives. In his strong name we pray. Amen.

CHAPTER 3

A Friend in Court

PSALM 7

I remember the phone call well. The teacher of my junior high Sunday school class was calling to talk to my mother. I had not done all my Sunday school lessons, and the teacher was putting pressure on my mother to bring me into line. I shook in my shoes as I craned my neck to overhear the conversation. To this day—and that's nearly thirty years now—I can feel the relief I experienced when my mother looked at my work and told the teacher that she thought it was pretty good for a boy in junior high.

My mother stuck up for me in a time of need. And I was grateful beyond words. She could be a strong disciplinarian, and one burning look from her flashing black eyes could wither any of her children. But here she was a friend in court. She felt that I was being unjustly accused, and she came to my defense.

Our psalm for today deals with just that kind of situation, and so do a number of the psalms. Listen as the psalmist in Psalm 7 pictures his predicament in prayer: "Save me from all my pursuers, and deliver me, lest like a lion they rend me, dragging me away, with none to rescue" (vv. 1, 2). Obviously he feels on the spot, hunted, stalked by those who seek to do him harm.

1. The Nature of the Problem

The precise nature of the problem surfaces in the next couple of verses: "O Lord, my God, if I have done this, if there is wrong in my hands, if I have requited my friends with evil or plundered my enemy without cause, let the enemy pursue me and overtake me . . ." (vv. 3-5). Here the accused psalmist protests his innocence. He denies his guilt, and the picture comes clear. He is being accused of a crime he did not commit. His enemies are conspiring against him, bringing charges of which he is innocent.

Now there is something that we must not miss here as we hear his words. The system of law in biblical times was utterly dependent on witnesses. The technical means of investigating crimes that we take for granted were unknown to the ancients. They knew nothing of fingerprints or hair types. They could not preserve footprints or produce photographs taken by hidden cameras. The elders in the city gates, where court was held, based their decisions largely on the words of witnesses.

Two biblical passages lend comment right here. Jesus said, "Out of the mouths of two or three witnesses every word shall be established" (Matthew 18:16). And even more familiar, "You shall not bear false witness against your neighbor" (Exodus 20:16).

So important were the words of witnesses in the Hebrew legal system that one of the Ten Commandments deals with them. Just as stealing, murdering, or committing adultery break the law of God and play hob with the tone of a society, so rigging a trial or denying justice undermine the life of God's people. Yet this is exactly what was happening to the psalmist. His standing in the community, his peace of mind,

23

his livelihood, his life itself were put in jeopardy by wicked witnesses and their stabbing lies.

2. The Danger of Aggressiveness

A sinful business this is—undercutting a person's confidence, tarring his character, jabbing at his reputation. One of the surest signs of our sinfulness is the way we persist in hurting other people.

The reasons for it are legion, I suppose. We push others down to make ourselves seem taller. Or we hang the blame on someone else to save our own necks. This is an old trick, you know. When God came to Adam to find out what had gone awry in the garden, Adam tried to duck the question and let it hit Eve: "It was that woman you gave me," Adam said (Genesis 3:12).

This is a good illustration of how sin confuses and corrupts our thinking. We not only do wrong, but we try to pass the buck when we do. We are like the man who was caught red-handed in the chicken shed. When the farmer called, "Who's there?", he said, "There is nobody here but us chickens." Sinners unwilling to take the rap—that's what we are. We swing back and forth from promises that we cannot keep to excuses that we cannot defend.

A psalm like this is always in season because it reminds us of our proneness and our power to wound others. It also reminds us that we should watch our tongues, squelch rumors, squash gossip, make sure that we have our facts straight. How many people have been hurt, how many churches have been divided, how many schools or Christian agencies have been damaged by well-meaning people who did not know what they were talking about. Bearing false witness is a dangerous business.

3. The Folly of Defensiveness

But so is defending ourselves all the time. The psalmist had no one else on his side but God, yet he knew he was in good hands. "My shield is with God," he says, "who saves the upright in heart" (v. 10). God is the one who defends me. I need no one else. What a lesson for us to learn!

Defending ourselves comes as easily as blaming someone else. There are a lot of things wrong with being defensive, always protecting ourselves, sticking up for ourselves. It keeps us from facing our faults, for one thing, and makes us prickly in our relationships with others. The person whose first concern is to take care of himself does not make a very good friend. We remember how silent Christ was before his accusers, even when they signed his death warrant with their lies. He trusted God to defend him, and so should we.

4. God, the Just Judge

No need for us to lash out at those who seem to do us wrong. We can trust God to judge. Our judgment is often fogged with prejudice; God's is not. Our judgment is usually slanted in our favor; God sees things as they are. As our psalmist declares: "God is a righteous judge, and a God who has indignation every day" (v. 11).

One thing is sure: God hates sin and injustice worse than we do. Not that we should sit on our hands, if there's something that we can do to right a wrong. But even when we feel helpless we can trust God.

Our psalmist makes clear that those who sin won't get away with it. Sin may grow within a wicked person with the relentlessness of pregnancy (v. 14). But judgment is certain. The sinner "makes a pit, digging it out, and falls into the hole which he has made. His mischief returns upon his own head . . ." (vv. 15, 16). No need for us to defend ourselves or accuse someone else. God is the judge. He makes no mistakes and overlooks no items on his agenda.

When the curtain of history will ring down, God will have left no business unfinished. The judge of all the earth will do right. We don't need to accuse others, nor do we need to defend ourselves. God is our judge.

5. Christ, Our Friend in Court

This helpless Old Testament believer anticipates a New Testament truth: in Christ we have a friend in court, one who defends our cause continually. I like the way Paul rejoices over this in Romans 8:33-34: "Who shall bring any charge against God's elect?" That's the challenge Paul throws out. "It is God who justifies; who is to condemn?" Bring on your accusers, says Paul; God himself will deal with them. Paul is bold, almost brash as he celebrates our salvation.

Think of what it was like before we were Christians. We would sit in a small cell, or occasionally pace a step or two in our cramped quarters. In frustration we would clutch the bars and shake them. Then our turn in court would come. And with sweaty palms we would face the judge and all the evidence of our sin and failure.

But instead of steely eyes we see a look of mercy and find that somehow our penalty has been paid and our sentence waived. And we are free. We have a friend in court. Our accusers are put down.

Other people know our faults well; but God declares us to be righteous. Satan, the master accuser, would love to bog us down in our guilt, to get us to soak in despair over our failure; but God has justified us. Our conscience tries to dredge up from the dark channels of our past the wrecks of our rawness, our rudeness, our rebellion; but God is our savior. In Christ we have a friend in court.

Once when my father was a student over sixty years ago, some well-meaning men accused him publicly of some financial irregularity. The president of his university stood up and offered to return whatever money was involved because he had such confidence in my dad and his integrity. In a time of crucial need, my father had a friend in court.

And so do you. That's what the gospel is all about. God is our shield. We don't defend ourselves. We don't stoop to rationalize or excuse. God is our judge and defender. We can put our whole trust in him. In Christ, he calls us righteous, and he's never yet lost an argument.

Prayer: God, how great you are and how good. When we did not have a leg to stand on you stood up for us. When we were caught red-handed you defended us. Thank you for such a great salvation. Through Jesus Christ we pray. Amen.

CHAPTER 4

The Glories and Limitations of Man

PSALM 8

What do you think of when you go out for a walk at night? You see the moon and the stars, the bright bulb and those 10,000 pin pricks of light. How do you react? Some people get romantic and long to hold hands with a loved one. Others with a scientific bent think of quasars and super novae and speculate on how long light takes to get here. In increasing numbers today people are looking at the stars as guides to life and making their decision by the positions of the planets. But the psalmists were neither romantics, scientists or astrologers.

When a psalmist strolled at night and gazed at the beauty of the Palestinian countryside, his eyes were lifted heavenward. To him the moon and the stars revealed the majesty of the God who spoke them into existence and whose fingers flicked them along in their courses. He thought of the great gap between God and man and the grace of God that bridged that gap.

This is what he said, "When I look at thy heavens, the work of thy fingers, the moon and the stars which thou hast established; what is man that thou art mindful of him and the son of man that thou dost care for him?" This is the response of a man of faith, and we find it in Psalm 8. He knows who made the stars, and he knows who made and cares for man. Scarcely any passage in Scripture sets out more clearly the glories of man and yet his limitations as well. Psalm 8 is our text. It's one of the psalms for all seasons.

When we looked at Psalm 1 we found it to be a psalm for undisciplined days. In it we saw that we must shun the ways of evil people, while at the same time we try to show them the love of God. We don't copy their example, but we don't reject them or disassociate ourselves from them. And we saw that to delight in God's law is not to be fettered with legalism but to do his will in response to his love and to his grace. As Christians, we obey the law not to please God, but because he has already accepted us in Jesus Christ.

The theme verse of Psalm 8 is tremendously important. It's the verse with which the psalm begins and closes. "O Lord, our Lord, how majestic is thy name in all the earth." We shall undersell man's glory and overlook his limitations unless we bear this verse in mind.

1. Glories of Man Received from God

The first point we want to see from this psalm is that **the glories of man are received from God himself.** You might call Psalm 8 a commentary on the first two chapters of Genesis, that magnificent account of the creation of man. Genesis and this psalm underscore a crucial idea: man is only man in relationship to God. Now this is hard for us to take in. It tends to stick in our throats on the way down. We want to be men on our own, to take credit for what we have achieved. We would love to win the award for the self-made man of the year. But when we think that way we are caught up in classic arrogance. We are gripped by a cosmic insolence that the Bible continually denounces.

Man is only man in relationship to God. This is the verdict of the Scriptures no matter where we turn. Man is made by God and for God. His purposes are given by God. His life is sustained by God. His destiny is judged by God. Only the fool tries to live as if his life did not hang on the grace and care of God almighty.

The psalmist knew well man's power and his potential. He does not sell us short, but he knows where the power and potential come from. "Thou hast made him a little less than God," the psalmist says, "and dost crown him with glory and honor. Thou hast given him dominion over the works of thy hands. Thou hast put all things under his feet" (vv. 5, 6). This is a summary of the uniqueness of man, who is related to God in a way different from anything else in creation. And this passage is a digest of man's God-given purpose: to take charge of the creation and to put it to use for God's glory.

But notice that God is the subject of all the verbs. Man's station has not been the result of man's achievement but of God's command: thou hast made; thou dost crown; thou hast given; thou hast put. And this is where the emphasis must be. Man has glory. He's important. He's the crown of creation. He has abilities that no other creature knows anything about. But all these abilities and aptitudes are gifts of God. Let's never forget it.

Two men were looking at the stars and musing on the vastness of space. And, thinking of the vast ranges of the cosmos, the years that it took that light to reach his eyes on earth, one man said, "Astronomically speaking, man is insignificant." The other man corrected him: "Astronomically speaking, man is the astronomer."

Only man can study the stars. We study them; they don't study us. We look out through our telescopes, but we have never yet seen anyone looking back at us. The glories of man, yes; but the glories of man are the gifts of God. "O Lord, our Lord, how majestic is thy name in all the earth." That's the message of the psalmist.

2. Glories of Man Ruined by Rebellion

But there's a second point that we have to put across, as we deal with the glories and the limitations of man: **the glories of man are ruined by our rebellion.** Now Psalm 8 comments on Genesis 1 and 2, but not on Genesis 3, which tells us that, in seeking our full freedom, we lost the freedom we had. I say we, by the way, when I talk about the fall, because we were all involved. The full impact of what the first man did leaves its mark all over us.

The author of Hebrews has some pointed observations to make on Psalm 8 just in this area; let's hear them. "As it is," he says, "we do not see everything in subjection to him" (Hebrews 2:8). Not all things are now under man's feet. In fact man seems to be swamped by life instead of being on top of it. When man refused to be man on God's terms, his glory was tarnished and his authority over creation was sharply curtailed.

God had given man great freedom, "Of every tree in the garden you may freely eat," he was told

(Genesis 2:16). Yet God has set limits to man's freedom to remind him continually that man is not God. But man wanted to rewrite the rules. He yearned for what he thought would be full freedom, and he lost what he had.

This moving account of the creation and fall of man is God's own explanation of man's potential and of man's problems. Next to the gospel of Jesus Christ, it is the most important piece of literature known to the human family.

Our relationship to the creation turned sour. This is one result of man's rebellion. The thorns and thistles in the garden of Eden symbolize our problems.

Think of how much worse things are today. We build factories to provide jobs for our people and goods for our nation, but the factories pollute the waters of our streams and lakes. We use our earnings to buy automobiles to make it easier to get to work, and automobiles fill the air with poisonous gases. Our eyes burn, and our lungs are clogged with smog. In trying to do right, we do wrong. In trying to use the creation, we abuse it. Man the great discoverer is also man the great spoiler.

Man himself cannot be in full control, because man himself is out of control. That's the message of the Bible. His motives are fouled up; he grovels in the slime of life as though he were not made by God, or he tries to soar heavenly heights as though he were God himself.

In these two ways man parades his fallenness. He demeans and debases himself as though he were the scum of creation instead of its crown. He worships things and pins his hopes on them instead of God. Or he tries to play god for himself and others in his haughtiness and pride. Man is not what he wants to be.

Psalm 8 describes man as he was and as he should be. The utterly realistic writer in Hebrews shows what man in his sin has become. But he doesn't stop there. He knows the theme verse of Psalm 8, and he knows that this is still true: "O Lord, our Lord, how majestic is thy name in all the earth."

3. Glories of Man Recovered in Jesus Christ

The author of Hebrews says that we see **the glories of man recovered in Jesus Christ.** That's the third point for us to make. If we don't see all things now under man's feet, what do we see? Hebrews tells us plainly, "We see Jesus, crowned with glory and honor" (Hebrews 2:9). He is the true fulfillment of the description of man in the psalm. It's as though Christ himself sat for the portrait. In him all that God wants man to be is revealed.

Christ became flesh and blood so that he would understand our problems and cope with them. The will of God is the law of human life, as we saw in the first psalm. Our failure to realize this, or even more to practice it, is the source of all of our troubles. Christ could be crowned with glory and honor because he obeyed the will of God even when it meant suffering and death. The road to power and glory is not the road of grasping ambition but humble self-denial.

What the first man missed, Jesus has recovered. The two great enemies of man, which slithered into that first garden and have successfully stalked man ever since, are sin and death. There can be no bright hour, no shining day for man until these enemies are done in. There's no freedom for man where sin is master, and there's no glory for man where death is lord.

The cross was God's way of dealing with sin. The way back to God was clear. Full forgiveness was possible. But something else happened on the cross. Not only was sin dealt with, but death itself was defeated. God had warned man that when he sinned man would sign his own death warrant. Now in Christ, God put death to death.

In other words, Christ took the poison of death into himself and by his death created a vaccine or an antitoxin with which the poison of death could be combatted. Or to put it another way, like an attacking army, death put all its troops into the fray to destroy Christ. It put him to death but all its power was sapped in the massive assault. And now it has no power over us. By Christ's death and Christ's resurrection, sin and death have their backs broken and the way is open for man to enjoy the glory and authority he once had.

We're creatures, and we are sinners. We have glory as God's creatures, and yet we have limitations. But Christ is Lord; this is the thing to remember; and by faith we participate in his victory. Because of what Jesus has done, the words of the psalmist are more true than ever: "O Lord, our Lord, how majestic is thy name in all the earth."

All that man was meant to be and will ever be has already been realized in Jesus Christ. He is Lord of all creation. All things are under his feet including the worst enemies of man: sin and death. And when we trust him, his victory becomes ours.

Prayer: Help us, our Father, to know where we have missed but where Jesus Christ has made it for us. Forgive our foolish, feverish efforts to solve problems which only you can deal with. Teach us to tear up our false definitions of what it means to be human and to write your description in large letters on our hearts and minds. Through Jesus Christ we pray. Amen.

CHAPTER 5

What the Nations Need to Know

PSALM 9

The annals of history are crammed with the records of what nations have achieved. Political organization has yielded astounding results. The Sumerians, for instance, who lived more than five thousand years ago, built systems of irrigation that took full advantage of the seasonal flooding of the Tigris and Euphrates rivers. And they developed patterns of government to regulate the water rights and the canal maintenance.

About the same time, the Egyptians mobilized huge numbers of people and vast amounts of material to build tombs for their kings—**pyramids** we call them. These magnificent monuments are so colossal and so precisely made that we still don't know how they were built. The enormous cut stones fit within a fraction of an inch of each other and are laid level and square despite the fact that they weigh several tons each. They are an incredible achievement, demonstrating what can be done when a nation rallies its resources around one goal.

And what about the architecture of Greece or the Roman roads and aqueducts? These sturdy and graceful tributes to national endeavor still command our attention in this age of airports that sprawl around the suburbs and skyscrapers that stretch tall above our cities.

And modern nations have logged an enviable record of achievements. Brazil, for instance, has built an entirely new capital city, a city of breath-taking beauty and splendor. India has made great strides in agricultural and industrial development in the more than twenty years since she gained her independence. Israel has transformed long stretches of wilderness into fertile, fruit-producing farm land. Japan has multiplied its massive factories that flood the world with everything from transistor radios to sports cars. And the United States has mustered the energy and skill to send several sets of her citizens to the moon and back.

Yet all of these national achievements—whether technological or educational, political or cultural—can be deceptive. Nations that have both attempted and accomplished so much can unknowingly lure themselves into thinking that they are self-sufficient, that they are laws unto themselves. They may develop the mistaken idea that they generate their own resources, write their own rules, and determine their own destinies.

Psalm 9 is surely a psalm for a time like ours, a psalm for **all** seasons, in fact. It lays out in no uncertain terms what all nations need to know. The psalm becomes more intriguing when we realize it is a king who does the speaking. A seasoned political leader in Israel lifts his voice to God in prayer and, as he does, gives the soundest political advice any nation could want to hear. He urges God to teach the nations to fear him and then draws his prayer to a close with "Let the nations know that they are but men!" (v. 20).

In the midst of his power, prestige, and authority, this king of Israel knew the difference between God and himself—a crucial lesson for all of us to learn. The wise king knew that political might had severe limitations, limitations that any nation would do well to reckon with.

1. Grateful for God's Provision

The king's impassioned prayer contains impressive insight into the attitudes national leaders should cultivate if they are to avoid the arrogance and insolence that so often mark their disposition. Gratitude for God's provision is the first course in the curriculum that the nations need to take, a curriculum designed to teach them that they are but men.

The psalmist demonstrates this as he begins his prayer: "I will give thanks to the Lord with my whole heart; I will tell of all thy wonderful deeds. I will be glad and exult in thee, I will sing praise to thy name, O Most High" (vv. 1, 2). The specific context of the king's gratitude is deliverance from the pressure that enemy nations had brought to bear on him. The exact historical setting is not apparent in the psalm. But the predicament was certainly an agonizing one: "Be gracious to me, O Lord! Behold what I suffer from those who hate me, O thou who liftest me up from the gates of death, that I may recount all thy praises, that in the gates of the daughter of Zion I may rejoice in thy deliverance" (vv. 13, 14). The king's great suffering (he was carried to "the gates of death") sparks deep gratitude when he is delivered.

The fact that he prays at all is a sign of his dependence on God. The fact that his prayer begins with thanksgiving frames the perspective from which he looks at all of life. The fact that he openly acknowledges that he, with all his political and military power, could not rescue himself shows how qualified he is to teach others the way of faith.

To live in faith is to give thanks. Not to give thanks is to declare our independence from God and expose ourselves as pagan. The nations need to know that they are but men, men who ought to be grateful to God for his provision.

2. Obedient to God's Commandments

Israel's good and wise king not only demonstrates the gratitude that should be the hallmark of all men, but he also stresses the obedience to God's commandments that is another key attitude of those who are truly human. The nations that have vexed him with their cruelty and oppression have made a great mistake. They are not merely politically indiscreet; they have not merely broken international agreements with their ruthless violation of boundaries; they have sinned against God. The psalmist puts it even more dramatically: "The wicked shall depart to Sheol, all the nations that forget God" (v. 17). Forgetting God means acting as though he did not exist, laying our plans as though he were not concerned, forming our values without consulting him, disregarding the rights of others as though they were not important to him.

The nations forgot God, and, when they did, lots of other things went wrong. A studied disregard of human rights and dignity crept into their thinking. Forgetting God, they lost sight of how important men were—that is, men who did not fit their perverted priorities and values. The political powers that were commissioned by God to enforce justice in society became specialists in injustice.

Almost nothing vexes God more or rouses his zeal to judge more than the flagrant disregard of human rights, especially the rights of those who do not have the political or economic strength to care for themselves: "For the needy shall not always be forgotten, and the hope of the poor shall not perish forever" (v. 18).

Let the nations know that they are but men, men who must be obedient to God's commands.

3. Responsible to God's Judgment

For those who do not obey, the result is clear: judgment. The psalmist says a lot about it, but his approach is different from ours. He looks forward to judgment and rejoices in it ahead of time: "But the Lord sits enthroned for ever, he has established his throne for judgment; and he judges the world with righteousness, he judges the peoples with equity" (vv. 7, 8). And again the king praises God: "For thou hast maintained my just cause; thou hast sat on the throne giving righteous judgment" (v. 4). It is the **restorative** aspect of judgment that is celebrated here. Part of what God does when he judges is to redress grievances, to right wrongs, to reward those of steadfast faith and stalwart conduct. In other words, the psalmist really trusts God. Along the way it may often appear that evil has the upper hand and that good deeds go unnoticed. But righteousness and equity are the style of God's judgment. We can bank on him always to do right, though his schedule and timing may not always coincide with ours.

But there is a **retributive** aspect of judgment as well. Where God is not worshipped as God, where men are not honored as men—and remember that the Bible commands us to "honor all men" (I Peter 2:17)—judgment must be the result. Often in biblical pictures of judgment the punishment fits the crime. The nations forgot God, and he in turn has "blotted out their name for ever and ever" (v. 5). The evil that they schemed against others has boomeranged against them: "The nations have sunk in the pit which they made; in the net which they hid has their own foot been caught" (v. 15).

As long as God is God, judgment is inevitable. As long as man is man, he is totally responsible to God, his righteous judge. Let the nations know that they are but men, men who whether they like it or not are responsible to God in judgment.

For us not to know that we are men does not enhance our manhood; it diminishes it. To try to be more than human always ends up making us less than human. What the nations, what all of us within the nations, need to know is that God is God and we are men. Obedience not power should be our ambition; worship not exploitation should be our way of life.

Prayer: Lord, we remember how Jesus was once offered all the kingdoms of the world in exchange for worshipping Satan. And we remember that he turned the proposition down as a bad deal. Teach us his values and help us to see all kingdoms from his perspective. He worshipped you and you alone. And that's what we really want to do. Help us to do it better, through his grace and his power. In the name of Jesus, who is King of kings, we pray. Amen.

CHAPTER 6

The Fool's Affirmation

PSALM 14

The word fool is never used lightly in the Bible. In fact, Jesus himself warns us strongly against branding anyone a fool: "But I say to you that every one who is angry with his brother shall be liable to judgment; whoever insults his brother shall be liable to the council, and whoever says, 'You fool!' shall be liable to the hell of fire" (Matthew 5:22). The Bible's belief in human dignity sternly discourages any loose use of the word fool.

Therefore, we must take the psalmist's statement with great seriousness when he says, "The fool says in his heart, 'There is no God'" (v. 1). To get the full point of this passage we must understand what **fool** means. A fool is not a person who lacks information. Ignorance we can treat sympathetically because the possibility of learning is always present where there is a will to learn. We don't fault people for not knowing what they have not had opportunity to learn.

A fool is not a person who lacks intelligence. We should be patient with slow learners and lead them along at their own pace. Dullness of mind is no virtue, but it is certainly not a vice for which people stand condemned.

A fool is not a person who merely **lacks** judgment. Silliness and foolishness do not mean the same thing in biblical language. People mature at different speeds and must be allowed to do so with gentle encouragement and long-suffering.

A fool is something different, as the Bible sees him. He is stubborn, set, and dogged in his commitment to rebellion and disobedience. He has plenty of information, but refuses to act on it. He may be highly intelligent, but he uses his intelligence to rationalize wrong conduct. He may be mature, as men measure maturity, but he uses his maturity to reinforce willfully wicked attitudes and perverted living.

For the psalmist, the essence of foolishness is to act as though God does not exist. I say **act** because it is practical atheism not theoretical atheism the psalmist has in view. It is not a finely reasoned debate about the existence of God, but the flagrant refusal to take God's existence seriously.

The foolish attitude described in Psalm 14 is the exact opposite of committed faith pictured in Hebrews 11:6: "And without faith it is impossible to please him [God]. For whoever would draw near to God must believe that he exists and that he rewards those who seek him." Mere intellectual assent to God's existence is not enough. Belief in God means staking our lives on his existence, and living every moment in terms of this commitment. This is precisely what the fool does not do.

1. Corruption in Conduct

Turning his back on God, even thumbing his nose at him, he gives himself to all manner of corrupt conduct. There can be no doubt that what we believe will profoundly shape how we live. Adolf Hitler believed that the Jewish race threatened the purity of German society, so he systematically, relentlessly, and efficiently exterminated millions of Jews. What he believed he acted upon. His distorted ideas resulted in dastardly conduct.

Likewise for fools. Denying God, they think they're free to write their own rules, fix their own values, and set up their own standards. The results are dreadful: "They are corrupt, they do abominable deeds, there is none that does good" (v. 1).

These results are not immediately evident. Many people ignore God while trying to maintain standards of courtesy, decency, and justice. For a while they appear to succeed. But sooner or later their false beliefs catch up with them. Without a firm commitment to God it is impossible to maintain standards of righteousness.

When we allow our conduct to be governed by the changing, shifting, and relative norms of society, we become openly vulnerable to our sinful urges and to the perverted patterns of our culture.

Firm commitments to righteousness, alert vigilance regarding sin, and passionate concern for human good freely flow from responsive faith in the living God. The moral outcome of rejecting God has such grave consequences that the psalmist presses the point by expanding his description of the non-believing fool: "They have all gone astray, they are all alike corrupt; there is none that does good, no, not one" (v. 3).

2. Indifference in Worship

The bitter perverseness that produces corrupt conduct also provokes a neglect of worship. The flagrant declaration of independence from God is complete. The fool shows no regard for good or God. This, of course, is the essence of foolishness. God created him in the beginning, sustains him along the way, and will hold him accountable at the end. Yet he pretends, fool that he is, that God does not exist.

The psalmist hints at the irony of this when he notes that "The Lord looks down from heaven upon the children of men" (v. 2). You can feel the contrast: the Lord in heaven, surrounded by power and glory, might and majesty; the children of men on earth, marred by frailty and futility, impotence, and corruption—yet they ignore him.

The purpose of this divine inspection is to determine who are wise enough to worship, to seek after God. Wisdom and worship are equated just as foolishness and rebellion are equated.

The wise man worships because he knows his crucial need for forgiveness. The fool is indifferent to worship and cuts himself off from access to the God who forgives. What he needs most, he deliberately deprives himself of by not seeking the Lord. He either deceives himself by thinking he has not sinned or lulls himself into believing it makes no difference.

The wise man worships because he knows that his knowledge of goodness and truth comes from God. By reminding himself regularly of what God is like, he confirms and corrects his understanding of what he ought to be. The fool goes it alone and, consequently, goes wrong. The wise man knows that by God's standard he will be judged, and he seeks to live accordingly. The fool believes there are no standards, and proceeds to demonstrate his beguiling belief through his corrupt conduct.

3. Hostility in Relationships

The matter does not end with the fool's wretched conduct or his religious indifference. Apparently, he proceeds to make it difficult for all who differ from him in faith and life. Perhaps his feelings of guilt and empty rebellion goad him to act hostilely towards the wise whose piety exposes his skepticism. He is so firmly entrenched in his unbelief that he rejects all who disagree.

Biting enmity is the result. "Have they no knowledge, all the evildoers who eat up my people as they eat bread, and do not call upon the Lord?" (v. 4). A terrible harvest is reaped from the seed of unbelief! Not only futility for themselves, but also hardship for those who seek to live by faith. No love, no grace, no respect—just a life of bitterness and persecution.

Dire results like these do not always come. The fact that they sometimes do ought to raise the yellow flag of caution in all our minds. Playing fast and loose in our relationship to God is dangerous business. Our potential to hurt people, especially good people, is always great without it being aggravated by our rejection of God. Not to honor God who created man places us in fatal jeopardy of forgetting who man is and why he must be honored—not exploited.

The attitudes of the psalmist in all this are notable. Not a touch of envy creeps in. He is never tempted to taste the fools' menu. He is well aware of their fate: "There they shall be in great terror, for God is with the generation of the righteous" (v. 5). It is pity not spite that he feels. Implicit in what he says is the wish that the fool would cast rebellion aside, scrap his foolishness, and seek after God who is seeking him.

Furthermore, the continual opposition of the cynics has not shaken his own confidence in God's deliverance. At any given moment it may look as though all things are going badly and evil has the upper hand. But life's last words belong to God, and they are words of salvation and victory.

The psalmist's conclusion is both a prayer and an affirmation—that God will rescue his people and replace their anxiety with gladness. "O that deliverance for Israel would come out of Zion! When the Lord restores the fortunes of his people, Jacob shall rejoice, Israel shall be glad" (v. 7).

Skepticism was branded **foolish** in the Old Testament. What term is possibly strong enough to describe it now that Jesus Christ has given us so many reasons to believe? The psalmist had full confidence in God. How much more should we have, now that Jesus Christ has given us full assurance of God's love and power?

Prayer: Lord, mark us among the wise who give themselves to you in love and worship. Remind us of the richness of your ways amidst all the bargain-sale advertisements that seek to lure us to self-service. Whatever we are, keep us from being fools who bank on our own wisdom. Then make us wise enough to lean only on you. For Jesus' sake. Amen.

CHAPTER 7

A Happy Choice

PSALM 16

What do you think the results would be if we con-
ducted a poll among our friends and neighbors to
discover their attitude toward the Christian faith?
The responses would undoubtedly be mixed. "It's
okay for those who want to believe in it." "I don't
buy all that stuff about the supernatural—not in our
technological, scientific age." "Religious faith is prob-
ably helpful for little children; it gives them values.
And it may be good for old people, bringing them
hope and comfort."

Among the answers are bound to be statements
like these: "I would not mind becoming a Christian,
but I'm having too much fun to do so just now." Or,
"To follow the teachings of the Bible is too harsh and
rigorous for me. I want to do my own thing." And
again, "Think of all I'd have to give up if I really
turned my life over to God."

Psalm 16 is a psalm for all seasons because it
speaks directly to these attitudes and feelings. It
reminds us that outsiders are not always best qualified to judge the cost of believing in God. David and
the other psalmists speak as insiders, men of faith,
witnesses to keen commitment. And they do not
share these negative attitudes toward unreserved allegiance to God.

They know better, for they have taken a good look at the other choices in life and found them wanting. A life built upon faith in God has its difficulties. This we know. It is demanding in time, discipline, energy, money. It is restricting in conduct and activity. We can't do or say anything we want to. But compared with any other way of life, it is rewarding beyond measure. That's why people like the psalmists who really know God are ready at a moment's notice to talk about him. They know that life demands that we make a choice, and they see their surrender to God as a happy choice.

"Those who choose another god multiply their sorrows" is the firm, blunt way the psalmist says it (v. 4). In marked contrast, he goes into great detail to describe the delights he enjoys in depending upon God. "The Lord is my chosen portion and my cup" (v. 5). Better than a banquet, more desirable than fine food and drink is the psalmist's relationship to God. Knowing God nourishes his soul and refreshes his spirit: "The Lord is my chosen portion and my cup."

The psalmist is thoroughly willing to place his destiny in God's hand: "Thou holdest my lot" (v. 5). This is no blind commitment to chance, no casual shrugging off of responsibility by singing "Qué será será, whatever will be will be." It is the sure affirmation that the God who loves him and in whom his spirit takes full delight really does care for him and will do so till the end.

The psalmist's hope for the future is grounded in his experience during the past and the present. He has ample evidence that God intends good for him: "The lines have fallen for me in pleasant places; yea, I have a goodly heritage" (v. 6). The word pictures here are drawn from the realm of real estate. The poet compares his life with a land transaction. Let's suppose an elderly father owns a large tract of land that he wants to divide among his sons. Some of the land is rocky and desolate, while other parts are fertile, covered with rich topsoil and watered by pleasant streams. Some of the sons will get the good land and some will not. What David is saying is that God has given him a good life indeed. The boundaries of his living have kept him from harsh and desolate circumstances. His whole experience has been a rich legacy from God.

No wonder he draws this contrast: "Those who choose another god multiply their sorrows." When it comes to satisfaction, idols have nothing to offer. The psalmist has made a happy choice, and he joyfully sticks with it.

1. Confident in God's Counsel

After these exuberant exclamations of his delight in God, the psalmist lists three specific reasons for his happiness: he is confident in God's counsel; he is secure in God's protection; he is enriched by God's fellowship.

"I bless the Lord who gives me counsel; in the night also my heart instructs me" (v. 7). From the beginning man has needed help deciding what to do. The ancients had an appalling number of means for getting advice. Divining rods, ouija boards, cloud formations, fish livers—all these and more were consulted faithfully when tough decisions had to be made. And there were priests and soothsayers, wizards and witch doctors, old wives and fortune-tellers who made good livings dispensing advice to perplexed people.

No wonder the psalmist could take confidence in the counsel God gave him. How different it was to have the sure word of God given in the law, a word of which his conscience could remind him even in the loneliness of night. One thing is certain. No idol had ever spoken to its worshippers words of counsel or comfort. No false religion had ever held out to its followers the sound advice that the true, the living God has revealed in his word.

Many men and women today crave good counsel. Doctors' offices are jammed, psychologists' appointment books are filled weeks ahead, Dear Abby and Ann Landers are swamped with letters. Lonely and confused people, dazed by the complexities of life, are flocking to find counsel. And a great many are helped by it. But on the deepest issues of life—questions like Who am I? and What should I do with my life?—it is God's counsel in which we take confidence and by which we check all other advice.

2. Secure in God's Protection

But life is not only confused for us, it is downright dangerous. We need more than advice; we need protection. Disease, disaster, and death stalk our fallen world as dreaded enemies. None of us dares meet them on our own. "I keep the Lord always before me; because he is at my right hand, I shall not be moved" (v. 8). The man of faith knows that God is with him, because he seeks to go with God. And he is secure in God's protection, knowing that God has the power to put down even the worst enemies that make it their aim to do him in.

"Therefore my heart is glad, and my soul rejoices; my body also dwells secure" (v. 9). What a picture of poise this is. Unharried, unrattled, the believing man faces life kept by the knowledge that God's love and power combine to take care of him. Granted, the psalmists knew that not everything in life worked out as they thought it should. Bad things do happen to good people. But their faith resolutely weathered these grievous circumstances because the psalmists knew that tragedy was not the result of God's neglect or weakness but in some way was linked to his loving purposes.

They did not—and we do not—need to dart through life from bush to bush, hiding in the underbrush and then dashing for the next place of cover, looking over each shoulder as we go. We walk boldly, secure in the knowledge that the God who loves us is also able to take on our sternest foes. Do you know any idol, any false religion that can match that?

3. Enriched by God's Fellowship

More than protection is involved in knowing God. God is not merely a grim guard riding shotgun on the hurtling stagecoach of our living, defending us against those who would rob us of goods and gold. He is a friend whose very presence lends light to our lives. "Thou dost show me the path of life; in thy presence there is fulness of joy, in thy right hand are pleasures for evermore" (v. 11).

"Go with God; you'll thoroughly enjoy the trip!" That's what the psalmist is saying. Not only will God save you from false steps and foolish stops along the way, but his presence, his companionship, and his fellowship will prove to be sheer delight—downright pleasure! He knows what life is really like, and one of his goals is to immerse us in its full meaning.

"Those who choose another god multiply their sorrows . . . The Lord is my chosen portion and my cup." What a happy choice it is to go with God!

The teachings of Psalm 16 suggest several specific

conclusions about biblical faith. First, it is **personal.** We are persons. God is the person, the one in whom all that we mean by personality exists in fullest measure. He's not a vague force or mysterious influence but a person who gives us counsel, provides for our care and protection, and calls us to rich friendship with himself.

Second, biblical faith is **practical.** Our deepest needs are met; our sorest hurts are healed. In our confusion, God points the way out. In our fear, God shows himself strong. In our loneliness, God says, "Come with me."

Third, our biblical faith is **satisfying.** "Pleasant," "goodly," "glad," and "secure" are faith's adjectives. And "life," "joy," and "pleasures" are its nouns. Idolatry, empty religion, leads inevitably to multiplication of sorrows; faith in the living God brings a wonderful fulness of joy.

Finally, biblical faith is **exclusive.** No one can taste the goodness of God until he declares with the psalmist: "I say to the Lord, 'Thou art my Lord; I have no good apart from Thee'" (v. 2). True happiness demands that we choose between false worship, whatever form it may take, and the one true God who has come to us in Jesus Christ. But that is no harsh and fearful choice. Alongside the futile and harmful options of life, it is a happy choice indeed.

Prayer: Our Father, remind us of the command that your apostle John left to all men of faith: "Little children, keep yourselves from idols." Teach us what a happy, loving command this is. And help us to forget our idols as we look at your son, Jesus Christ, in whom all your fullness dwells. Give us the wisdom not to cling to false and foolish hopes but to open ourselves to full life, to abundant joy in Jesus. We ask these things because his love and grace have taught us how. Amen.

CHAPTER 8

For His Name's Sake

PSALM 23

In a popularity contest among the psalms, Psalm 23 would win hands down. How do we account for the perennial attraction that these six short verses have held for people everywhere?

For those of us reared on the King James Version, its peerless English may help to explain the lasting impact of this psalm. We would be hard pressed to find more telling examples of simple, clear, and forceful language than, "The Lord is my shepherd, I shall not want"; or, "Surely goodness and mercy shall follow me all the days of my life" (vv. 1, 6).

For many the sense of comfort derived from the psalm makes it memorable. By sick beds and at funerals, in times of emotional discouragement or financial depression, this psalm—more than any other part of Scripture—is read and heard.

For some, the attraction of the psalm may be nostalgia. It may evoke memories of home and family, of childhood days in church and Sunday school. We may recall the warm satisfaction of memorizing these lines for the first time and the continual comfort enjoyed in periodically rehearsing them through the years. Our friends in Scotland, where the psalms are always in season and are frequently sung in church services, have a particularly fond attachment to Psalm 23; it's virtually their national anthem.

Underlying these reasons for the enduring popularity of the shepherd psalm is one crucial factor: this psalm tells us about God in terms we can readily understand, in language and metaphors that make vivid impressions on our minds and hearts. It is the inspiring picture of God in all his goodness and glory that accounts for the memorable quality of the psalm. Here God is not remote and unapproachable, not withdrawn and inaccessible; he is "**my** shepherd" tending to **my** most pressing needs; he is **my** host extending lavish hospitality to **me** as his guest.

God is the hero of the entire Bible. Its pages show who God is and what he has done for us. And in a remarkable way Psalm 23 compresses into a few verses two of the great qualities of God's character: his goodness and his glory. Here we see him as he is and learn to love him as we ought.

1. God's Goodness

"The Lord is my shepherd." These words are startling both in their simplicity and their brashness. The psalmist is claiming that the God of heaven and earth, who rules the destiny of men and angels, who defeated the Egyptian pharaoh and rescued Israel from slavery, personally takes care of him. And he strengthens this bold affirmation with the claim, "I shall not want." God's care for him, God's goodness to him, is so constant, so thorough, so dependable that he lacks nothing.

He walks in "green pastures," in contrast with the bleak, harsh, stony terrain of Palestine. He rests beside "still waters," a relief from the scorching heat that blanches the countryside. No wonder his soul, his whole being, is refreshed! Sapped energies are replenished, and drained vitality is restored. All the provision and comfort sheep would want is abundantly furnished by the Shepherd God.

But there's more. Guidance and protection are also available. Twisting, tortuous paths beckon in all directions and threaten to lead us into blind corners and box canyons. But straight paths that lead to food and shelter are God's ways, and he helps us to find them. Valleys dark as death pose no puzzle to him or to us when he is there. He is equipped to protect his sheep, and we can continually take heart in his presence.

A good shepherd is what the psalmist calls his God, and the first four verses of the psalm describe God's gracious care. In the last two verses, however, the picture changes. Here God is depicted as a hospitable host who offers shelter and sustenance to weary travelers far from home. The same God, the same goodness, but a different word picture.

God spreads a table for his guests, and they eat to the full even though enemies stalk them in hope of ambush. The traditions of hospitality are strong in various regions of the world. In England and Scotland, for instance, hosts customarily serve an early morning cup of tea to their guests before breakfast, and sometimes they offer to polish their shoes. In India guests are often greeted with wreaths or chains of flowers as in Hawaii where floral leis and a kiss on the cheek are traditional.

In the ancient Middle East there were carefully guarded customs of hospitality. For example, the host was responsible for his guests' total welfare, including their physical protection if they were pursued by enemies. It is this custom that the psalmist draws upon as he describes the goodness of God.

"Thou anointest my head with oil" also recalls the ancient patterns of hospitality. Olive oil was frequently used to wash and refresh the hair and face of a dusty, grimy, chapped traveler arriving from his journey. To quench the traveler's thirst, the host furnished a cup so full of wine or water that it spilled when the guest tipped it to his lips. This custom underlies the psalmist's praise that "my cup overflows."

What grander, plainer, clearer way to picture God's love and grace, God's continual blessings and constant provision, than by comparing God to a noble, thoughtful host and us to his permanent guests. No wonder the psalmist shouts his exuberance when he exclaims, "Surely goodness and mercy shall follow me all the days of my life." This had been his experience up to now, and he confidently anticipates that it will continue. In fact, he expects to dwell with God forever. The fellowship has been so rich, the relationship so satisfying that he cannot imagine it ending. He has found life with the living God, and he asks nothing else but to enjoy that life with God forever.

2. God's Glory

The psalmist does more than describe God's goodness. He also gives the reason for God's lavish care of his people. This comes in a phrase at the end of verse 3 that we can easily overlook: "for his name's sake." There's a whole cluster of important ideas lodged in these four words. God's name, of course, stands for his person, his honor, his glory. A name in biblical thought is far more than a label; it is an expression of the character or personality of the individual. It stands for the person's very self—who he is and what he does.

This is why names are changed in the Bible when the nature of a person or his ministry changes. Abram becomes Abraham, the "father of a multitude"; Jacob becomes Israel after he wrestles with God and assumes a new role in God's program. And before his birth, Jesus is given a name that marks him as the savior: "And you shall call his name Jesus, for he will save his people from their sins" (Matthew 1:21).

"For his name's sake" means for the sake of all that God is and stands for. The simplest way to paraphrase this is to say "for his glory." This is simple, but it is not trite. God's glory has to be the profoundest idea in the universe. And since God is the supreme being of the universe, doing things for his name's sake is the greatest possible reason.

However, God not only leads us for his name's sake, he does everything else for this reason, too. His majestic acts of creation, his astounding deeds of salvation, and his careful provision for our most pressing needs—all these take place for God's glory, for his name's sake. To put it plainly, God's goodness stems from his glory.

God's purpose in creation and history is to make his glory known, to reveal himself so clearly as God that men and angels will join with the rest of creation in celebrating God's greatness and goodness, his majesty and might. In all that God does, his own reputation is at stake. He will not let himself down.

This is an assuring word. Our welfare, our security, our salvation, our destiny do not hinge on our ability. God has pledged himself to be our God in every sense of the word, and he will not back away from his commitment. Even when things seem to go wrong and God is not treating us in the way we would choose, we can trust him because he will always do what is best. And what is best for him is in the long run best for us. The expressions of God's goodness may change from time to time, but his concern for his glory is constant. God can never be less than God. In this we can continually take heart.

This is also a challenging word. If God lives to make his glory known, so should we. The greatest delight in life is to know God and to serve him, to do all that we do for his name's sake. This brings our purposes, which are so aimlessly directed, so readily misguided, and so infrequently fulfilled, into line with God's purposes. And that's the way we all really want to live.

Prayer: Our gracious God, what a good shepherd you are, guiding, providing, protecting, correcting. And what a thoughtful host. It's with you that we want to dwell and for you that we want to live. We are especially grateful that this is what you want, too. And we thank you for all you have done through your Son, Jesus Christ, to make this possible. In him we have learned more clearly what you are like, and through him we want to live for your glory. For his name's sake, we pray. Amen.

CHAPTER 9

The Blessings of Forgiveness

PSALM 32

The phone rings in a police station, and a forlorn voice says, "Come and get me." Piecing the bit of conversation together we find that for years the man has been harboring a secret. He stole a large sum of money from his employer, moved to another state and changed his name. He thought he had everything he wanted: freedom, wealth, leisure. But he failed to reckon on one fact. He laid his plans well and covered his tracks with skill. But he made a fatal miscalculation: he forgot about the power of conscience. And now he had to give himself up to keep from blowing his top.

We have all heard of dramatic incidents like this, but are we aware of what a guilty conscience can do to people who never make the headlines, people who carry their secrets like festering thorns that infect the whole personality? It would be hard to calculate the amount of damage done by guilt. A father or mother embittered by guilt and withdrawn from other members of the household can turn the whole family into a disaster area.

Guilt can make us edgy and nervous, scared that others may discover our secret. It can make us harsh and unappreciative or suspicious and distrusting, because we cannot really accept love from others.

We feel they will not really love us if they know how bad we are.

Only you know what guilt you live with and the toll it takes on your well-being. But if you felt personally touched by these words, there's a psalm which will apply directly to your situation: Psalm 32, another psalm which never goes out of date but applies in one way or another to all of us, a psalm for all seasons.

1. The Sordidness of Sin

There are two main ideas that hit us as we mull over the meaning of this psalm. The first is the sordidness of sin. Not a pleasant subject, but it is where we live. A lot of lines of evidence conspire to remind us of human sinfulness. Headlines, television dramas, novels, our contact with people and our own consciences combine to tell us that this is a fallen world, peopled with inhabitants who find it easier to do wrong than right.

One of the ways the psalmist uses to show the horror of sin is the variety of terms. The Hebrew language of the Old Testament has a rich vocabulary to describe the sorry sides of our human nature.

In the first two verses of Psalm 32 four words are used: transgression, sin, iniquity, deceit. Three of these are repeated in verse 5.

By **transgression** the psalmist means rebellion or mutiny. It's a word that would be used when soldiers turn against their commander and fail to obey his orders.

The term **sin** means to miss the mark, a word drawn from the field of archery. God's righteousness is like a target at which we take aim and usually miss. The prophet Hosea uses this figure in 7:16 when he calls Israel a "treacherous bow" or, as Phillips translates it, "they are like a bow which never shoots straight."

Iniquity means to twist away from God's path, to deviate from his standards and become crooked.

Deceit, of course, is the attempt to cover up all this wickedness, to pretend to be upright when we are crooked as a corkscrew.

Transgression, sin, iniquity, deceit. We are rebels who miss the mark, wander from the right path and try to cover our tracks. Not a happy set of attributes. We would not want them lettered on a certificate or carved on our tombstones. Yet they tell our story.

But the horror of sin is clear not only from the words used, but from the pangs of conscience so passionately expressed. Listen to verses 3 and 4: "When I declared not my sin, my body wasted away through my groaning all day long. For day and night thy hand was heavy upon me; my strength was dried up as by the heat of summer."

This passage scarcely needs comment. We can feel the inner agony, the burning heat of discontent and failure. The psalmist had ceased to function. No rest at night; no work by day. Worry derailed his train of concentration. Guilt sapped his energies. Soon his physical health was affected.

The Bible makes clear the close connection between problems of spirit and body. And modern medicine is finding out the truth of this. Think how terrible sin is that it tears us up like this.

But the psalmist's basic aim is not to remind us of the power of our enemy but to lift our eyes to the possibility of victory. Sin can be defeated. Not by us but by God.

2. The Fullness of God's Forgiveness

This victory is described in the second main idea of Psalm 32: the fullness of God's forgiveness. Again we note the range of words used. The variety of terms employed to describe our sin is matched by an equivalent set to depict God's forgiveness: **forgiven** means taken away. Sin is viewed as a burden to be removed, like garbage to be confined out of sight and smell. **Covered** means concealed, like a stain that mars and detracts. God is put out of sight. **Not imputed,** not reckoned, is a bookkeeping term. God does not credit sin to our account.

Part of the psalmist's picture of forgiveness is the place of confession. Confession is more than just getting sin off our chest. It is showing God how seriously we take it. The very repetition of the words sin, iniquity, transgression (v. 5), shows that the wrong is not being minimized. Seeking God's help and God's alone, the penitent writer bares his soul directly to the Lord, without argument or plea.

Following hard on the confession is the direct mention of forgiveness: "Then thou didst forgive the guilt of my sin" (v. 5). Throughout the psalm, parallelism and repetition have been used. We have seen that both sin and forgiveness are expressed in a variety of ways. The pangs of conscience are depicted in two verses, but the announcement of forgiveness is made in one line. This is the heart of the matter, and the psalmist puts it as directly and as simply as he can.

Throughout the psalm the central theme is **the God who forgives.** Let's not miss this. Our generation knows the importance of confession, the relief that comes from getting things off our chest. Psychology has taught us this. But biblical forgiveness is more. It is not only talking about our problems; it is telling **God** about them. He is involved in a way that no one else is. Whatever our sin, it is against God who made us and loves us. And because sin is against him, only he can forgive.

And he does forgive. That's the psalmist's point. Sin is terrible—it comes in all shapes and sizes. It catches us unaware, or we walk into it deliberately. It clutches us in a hundred different holds and seeks to pin us to the mat.

But God is able. There is no sin he cannot cope with. There is no sinner that he cannot restore. There is no life that he cannot turn from foolishness and frustration to fruitfulness and satisfaction. God forgives. And don't you ever forget it.

The God who forgives is a God who brings results. Two fruits of his forgiveness are found in Psalm 32:6-9. The first is a confidence to be enjoyed: "Thou art a hiding place for me, thou preservest me from trouble" (v. 7). The problem is dealt with, and we are free to trust God in all circumstances. The second fruit of forgiveness is a conviction to be shared: "I will instruct you and teach you the way you should go" (v. 8). This is not a private experience, but a personal one to be shared with God's people.

Perhaps the message of the psalm is best summed up in verse 10, "Many are the pangs of the wicked; but steadfast love surrounds him who trusts in the Lord." What a promise for those who trust God enough to seek and find his forgiveness!

Where sin is taken lightly, people are in real trouble. We talk about playing with dynamite or keeping a pet cobra in our kitchen. These are harmless experiences in comparison with courting sin. A lot of people are trying to get us to do just that. They claim that we have been inhibited, hung up, as they put it, by our Puritan background. They use glib words and cute arguments to try to get us to throw away our moral convictions. Don't believe them.

People may be able to polish their consciences so they look shiny, but if they have broken God's will the rust is still there under the surface. And the corrosion of guilt will eat away at their lives.

Believe God when he says through the psalmist that the answer is not silence and the solution is not rationalization, but forgiveness. You **cannot** hide your sin, and you **will not** forget it.

Level with God. Talk openly, squarely with him. He will forgive. The cross is his pledge. His word is his bond. The experience of the psalmist and millions like him is the evidence. Happiness begins with forgiveness and nowhere else.

Prayer: Our Father, don't let the anguish and the insight of the psalmist be wasted on us. We sense our common plight with his in our sinning. Teach us to share with him the delight of coming to terms with you. Through Jesus Christ we pray. Amen.

CHAPTER 10

The Relief That Comes
from Rescue

PSALM 40

Nothing excites a community like a rescue operation. Let a youngster get stuck in a well or buried in a cave-in, and the whole neighborhood will rally to meet the need. The fire department, police and a host of volunteers will be on hand with everything from searchlights to soup. And they should be.

Some of you live in mining communities. You know the shudder that goes through the town when someone is trapped in the mine shaft: the anxious waiting, the frenzied attempts to establish contact, the exhilaration of rescue, the unbridled joy of reunion. Another victim has escaped the clutches of that gloomy pit.

The Bible knows these emotions first hand. Psalm 40 expresses compellingly the relief that comes from rescue: "I waited patiently for the Lord; he inclined to me and heard my cry. He drew me up from the desolate pit, out of the miry bog, and set my feet upon a rock, making my steps secure" (vv. 1, 2).

Psalms For All Seasons is what we call this series of studies, and Psalm 40 certainly fits that title. It deals with problems we all face and expresses a de-

light that some of us have come to know—a delight in
God's deliverance from some sharp crisis.

1. A Perilous Predicament

We cannot be sure what the writer's predicament
was, but in verse 12 he tells us that evils without
number have encompassed him. "My iniquities," he
cries, "my iniquities have overtaken me till I cannot
see; they are more than the hairs of my head; my
heart fails me."

Apparently the psalmist was feeling the sting of
judgment for his failure to obey God. He had slipped
in a pit dug by his own hands. He was bogged down in
his own shortcomings; his feet were stuck in the mud
of his transgressions.

But more than that, he had enemies who were
enjoying his plight. They desired his hurt and even
sought to snatch away his life (v. 14). Not only was
the sufferer in a steep pit with his feet caught in wet
clay, but those who might have helped him were
kicking at the sides of the pit to cave it in on him.
They stepped on his fingers as he sought to pull
himself up.

Misfortune and suffering call for unusual compassion from those who surround the sufferer. No
one, no matter what he has done, deserves Job's
comforters—people who say, "I told you so," or who
gloat over the predicament of others.

But **God** heard the psalmist's plea and was ready
to forgive and to rescue. Up the slippery slopes he
pulled the man and set him on a firm place.

And God did not stop there; he even helped the
stunned man overcome his state of shock and express
his praise: "He put a new song in my mouth, a song
of praise to our God."

2. A Praise-Filled Response

We can be so blinded by sin, so embittered by suffering that we don't know how to thank God for what he has done. But God himself has given us words of praise in the psalter. He has written our new songs for us, and we should use them.

Learn to live in the Psalms and to make personal use of the prayer and praise that God has placed there for you. Whatever expression of spiritual emotion you need can be found among the 150 poems that form the center of the Bible. They are always in season.

In Psalm 40, the rescued man whose life had been trapped in sin and suffering is given a new song—a song of praise. This calls for comment because it stands for the core of what God is doing for his people.

Two questions come to mind as we listen to the response of the rescued believer: first, why a song; second, why a new song?

Singing a Song. God gives him a song because a song is the best way to express praise. A song is poetry. It appeals to the imagination. It uses figures of speech and word pictures. How else can we talk about God whom we have not seen and whose character is too grand to be described in ordinary language. The Bible itself uses poetry, especially in the Psalms and prophets, to describe the greatness and glory of God.

Singing his praise is important too because singing involves our whole person. It is hard to sing half-heartedly. Singing taxes us. It catches us up in the song with a zest that lifts us out of ourselves and loses us in the theme of our song and the joy of our singing.

When God does something great for us we don't recite a proverb, derive a formula, compose a paragraph, engage in debate, prepare a recipe. We sing a song. That's what believers have done through the ages.

Singing a New Song. But why a new song? The reason is clear: each time God rescues us is a new experience and demands a new song. In other words, God's acts of salvation throughout history are not mere routine repetition of what he has already done. They are new acts. History is moving on step by step, stage by stage, nudged and nurtured by God. Each grand event along the way calls for new response from his people, and that new response is a new song.

Think of Miriam's song when she and her people had crossed the sea and could look back on their former days of bondage (Exodus 15:20-21). Think of Hannah's song when she knew that Samuel was on the way (I Samuel 2:1-10). Think of Mary's song when she was told that she would bear the Christ (Luke 1:46-55). What new song should **you** sing as you thank God for rescuing you from the pit of meaninglessness and futility?

Sharing Our Relief. The new song is not only a channel of praise to God but a means of sharing our good news with others. The psalmist cannot keep his experience to himself. He has been rescued and his relief becomes public property: "I have told the glad news of deliverance in the great congregation . . . I have not restrained my lips . . . I have not hid thy saving help within my heart . . . I have not concealed thy steadfast love and thy faithfulness from the great congregation" (vv. 9, 10).

Why all this emphasis on sharing? Why is it not enough to thank God without involving the whole congregation? Three reasons can be given for this public expression of joy. The first is that it **increases the sense of rejoicing** for the one who was rescued. Half the satisfaction of something wonderful is being able to share it. I once traveled for six weeks in Europe by myself and literally suffered because I had no one to enjoy the sights with me. To stand at an historic shrine, to sit in a great opera house, to walk through a rich museum and have no one to talk things over with is a kind of torture.

When surprises come our way, when the mail brings good news, when the boss gives us a rise in salary, our first thought is to tell those close to us. The telling and retelling of our high moments keeps them bright before us. We relive them, savor their taste, relish their feel again and again. Begin to share day by day what God has done for you and you'll know what the psalmist meant.

Sharing our joys does more than enrich us; it also **encourages our friends.** All around are people who are lonely, bitter, discouraged, who feel that life has been drained of its meaning, that all hope has been wrung out of their lives. Let them know that God cares, that Jesus loves, that the Holy Spirit can be their comforter. Share your faith, your hope, your love. What God has done for you can be like a torch to light the hopes of others and set their lives ablaze with joy and purpose.

And one more thing: telling others what God has done **brings glory to God.** People may know that something good has happened, some dramatic change has taken place; but they don't know why. Unless we tell them, they may be tempted to misinterpret. "My, that was good luck," they may say. Or, "you sure were clever to work yourself out of that predicament." And they will miss the whole point.

God is at work, and we don't believe in luck. The height of sinfulness would be for us to take credit for what God has done. Both honesty and devotion demand that we give credit where credit is due—to God. Then "many will see and fear, and put their trust in the Lord" (v. 3).

3. The Praiseworthy Rescuer

What we want to learn most of all from this psalm is that God is the hero of our biblical faith. That's why this psalm is good for all seasons. It points us to the God who never changes.

Let's see what we can learn about God from Psalm 40. First of all, he's incomparable: "none can compare with thee," the psalmist shouts in verse 5 as he remembers that the Lord has so multiplied his good deeds toward man that they cannot be counted. It's hard for us to comprehend the uniqueness of God.

Much of our understanding is based on comparisons. We learn numbers by seeing that some are larger than others. We learn history by comparing events and circumstances in one era with those in another. We trace developments in art and architecture by setting various paintings or drawings side by side and spotting the similarities and differences.

But with whom can we compare God? He's one of a kind. And his uniqueness is part of his greatness. He can rescue us because he's not bound by our limitations. God is not just a little bigger and better than we. He's different. He's God, not man.

God is not only incomparable as the great rescuer of lost men; he is faithful to those who call upon him in time of need. Three times in these few verses the faithfulness of God is celebrated: "I have spoken of thy faithfulness and thy salvation. I have not concealed thy steadfast love and thy faithfulness . . . Let thy steadfast love and thy faithfulness ever preserve me" (vv. 10, 11).

Dependability is what lies at the heart of faithfulness. God is incomparable but not whimsical. He can be counted on. We may not understand everything that he does. He may work on his schedule not ours. But our basic difficulty is not God's reliability but our reluctance to rely on him.

He is faithful, and his faithfulness is expressed in steadfast love. When God chose Israel to be his people, he made a compact or covenant with them in which he pledged himself to be their God, and they swore that they would worship and serve him only. Through the centuries, despite Israel's rebellion and disobedience, God has more than stuck by his bargain. His love is not fickle; it does not blow hot and cold. **Steadfast** love is the way to describe it.

What a testimony this psalm is. Nothing theoretical here. The psalmist met God in the midst of a sorry predicament. And God showed his greatness, and not only his greatness but his compassion. "As for me, I am poor and needy; but the Lord takes thought for me" (v. 17). The psalmist found that to be true, and so can you.

Prayer: Thank you, Father, for hearing our cry, and for not turning your back on our deepest needs. Thank you for being dependable and able. Help us to know how much you care. Help us to see all that you have done for us in Jesus Christ, who has become the theme of our new song. Give us grace to sing it well. In Jesus' name we pray. Amen.

CHAPTER 11

A Royal Wedding

PSALM 45

The psalms are always in season because they cover such a wide range of subjects. All the deep emotions of our human spirit are vented by the psalmists: praise and thanksgiving, trust and dependence, dedication and devotion, surrender and commitment, questioning and argument, discouragement and despair, anxiety and anger.

All of the major experiences of life are commented on: birth and death, famine and plague, invasion and battle, political duties and social responsibilities, relating to our friends and raising our families, serving our God and obeying his Word. There's even a marriage ceremony recorded in the midst of the Psalter.

Psalm 45 is a song that celebrates the king's wedding. No specific king is mentioned, and it's very possible that this poem—or a variation of it—was used regularly at royal weddings. There are standard patterns that we follow in wedding ceremonies, and the people of Israel may have done the same.

Three reasons make it important for us to study this psalm. First, it gives an impressive picture of Israel's kings, and the esteem they receive from the people. Second, it helps us appreciate the beauty and glory of Christ, Israel's greater king. This psalm, like many, is partial preparation for his coming. Third,

Psalm 45 is a cogent reminder of the importance that marriage has in God's program for the human family. We habitually overlook the fact that when God made man in his own image, he also made him male and female. This sovereign act of creation places marriage at the heart of human life as God designed it.

For all these reasons—our understanding of Israel's great kingship, our appreciation for the greater king who came to rule us all, and our insight into the meaning of our own marriage—the time spent studying Psalm 45 is well invested. So let's begin.

1. Israel's Great King

For those of us raised in societies where we elect our leaders it is difficult to understand how highly the Israelites regarded their king. We tend to criticize or even lampoon our government officials at the slightest provocation. But Israel's king was held to be the father of the people, the embodiment of all their national achievements and aspirations.

Israel's government placed incredible responsibility on the king. Constitutional nations have developed checks and balances among the various branches of government—executive, legislative, judicial. But Israel's king was charged with all these duties and more. The government was **upon his shoulders** in the full sense of that phrase.

The king's central role is described in detail by the court scribe who provides the lovely wedding song in Psalm 45. After a brief word of admiration for the king's beauty, "You are the fairest of the sons of men" (v. 2), the scribe salutes the king's military prowess. He urges his stalwart leader to ride forth victoriously against his enemies (vv. 3-5).

One look at a map of the ancient Middle East

reminds us that Israel's king had to be skilled in the arts of warfare. Egypt and Assyria marched through Israel's terrain regularly in quest of power and wealth. Israel's near neighbors like the Philistines and Syrians, the Ammonites and Moabites, were constantly harassing their borders and plundering their countryside. The king's glory included his ability to protect his kingdom and defeat its enemies.

However, his success in international affairs depended on his righteousness at home. He was not only a warrior but also a judge charged with the maintenance of justice throughout the land: "Your royal scepter is a scepter of equity; you love righteousness and hate wickedness" (vv. 6, 7). God had given the law to his people with the stipulation that the rights of all citizens be safeguarded, and he commissioned the king personally to see that this was accomplished. For example, remember how Solomon himself decided the controversy between the two mothers who claimed the same baby (I Kings 3:16-28).

Weddings often remind us of the resource and responsibility of the bridegroom. Likewise, our poet remembers the royal bridegroom and reminds his hearers of what a good king can and ought to be. The key to the king's success is God's blessing. As the ruler responds to God's will and serves as God's representative among men, he is given wisdom and strength to live as God intended (vv. 7-9).

Though the scribe has concentrated on the king, the beauty and grace of the queen are praised in verses 10 and 15. All of us in middle age or beyond are tempted to give advice to young brides. The psalmist does not even try to resist the temptation: "Forget your people and your father's house; and the king will desire your beauty" (vv. 10, 11). The queens of Israel were often divided in their loyalty. However, their new duty and privilege was to honor their husbands and give their new home first allegiance.

2. The Church's Greater King

This wedding portrait, of a gallant king and his devoted wife, captures Israel's ideal hopes for their rulers. But their hopes seldom reached fruition in their kings. Power often turned the kings' heads, and the contacts with foreign lands corrupted their faith.

As king after king failed to meet God's standard, the wisest souls in Israel began to lift their eyes to the future. They trusted God to keep his promises and send a wonderful king—and send he did.

When the angel Gabriel revealed to Mary that she would give birth to Jesus, these were the words she heard: "He will be great, and will be called the Son of the Most High; and the Lord God will give to him the throne of his father David, and he will reign over the house of Jacob for ever; and of his kingdom there will be no end" (Luke 1:32-33).

And ever since, Christians have hailed Jesus as their king, often in language drawn from Psalm 45. Hymn writers, especially, have found a rich mine, and have set the stanzas of their songs with gems from this ancient psalm. "Majestic sweetness sits enthroned upon the Savior's brow; his head with radiant glories crowned, his lips with grace o'erflow." These lines together with another stanza that ends, "Fairer is he than all the fair who fill the heavenly train," are borrowed from verse 2: "You are the fairest of the sons of men; grace is poured upon your lips."

The Palm Sunday hymn "Ride On, Ride On, in Majesty" is based on verse 4: "In your majesty ride forth victoriously for the cause of truth and to defend the right." Likewise, verse 8 supplied the inspiration for the hymn "Ivory Palaces": "Your robes are all fragrant with myrrh and aloes and cassia. From ivory palaces stringed instruments make you glad."

In these descriptions of the beauty and splendor of Israel's king God has given prophecies concerning our greater king. A wedding hymn is very appropriate because Jesus called himself a bridegroom (Matthew 9:15). The apostle Paul speaks of the marriage of Christ to his church: "Husbands, love your wives, as Christ loved the church and gave himself up for her" (Ephesians 5:25). In the Book of Revelation John employs this theme and calls the great reunion of Christ and his people a wedding feast: "Blessed are those who are invited to the marriage supper of the Lamb" (Revelation 19:9). Of the church John writes, "and his Bride has made herself ready; and it was granted her to be clothed with fine linen, bright and pure" (Revelation 19:7-8).

3. Our Own Royalty

In these wedding pictures of Christ and his church we can easily overlook the lessons they hold for our marriage relationships. The greatest wedding in history, the central marriage in all of life, is Christ's love relationship with his church and her obedient loyal commitment to him. God's great purpose in creating the world and sending his Son was to bring this marriage about.

Your marriage and mine are part of this great program. Our calling is to reflect Christ's love, and the church's response to that love, in our own marriages.

Marriage is not just a convenient way for man and woman legally to live together, raise children, and enjoy each other's care and affection. Marriage has a deep spiritual purpose. It is God's way of demonstrating day after day in place after place the great secret of life: his love and our loyalty.

The Christian husband, as he spends himself in love and devotion to his wife, reminds all who know him of Jesus' greater love, love that pinned him to the cross. The Christian wife, in her faithful and gracious respect for her husband, demonstrates what the whole church—Christ's bride—is to be and do.

The light of God's word on marriage clears away the drabness and dullness that may have marred your relationship. As you come to know the meaning of Jesus' love you'll learn amazing lessons about your love. Giving yourself to Christ may not move you to easy street, but it will enable you to live in fine style wherever you are. Fine style, I say, because you too can live like royalty when your marriage is linked to the life and love of the King of kings.

Prayer: Heavenly Father, these are radiant pictures that you have shown us. Thank you for clarifying your love for us through Jesus Christ. Help us truly to give ourselves to each other as husbands and wives, and use us to demonstrate your love to others. All of our marriages need improvement and some need to be completely remodeled. Your Word has given us a good start; now enable us to continue in its light. We pray through Jesus Christ, who loved his Bride and gave himself for her. Amen.

CHAPTER 12

The Foolishness of False Trust

PSALM 49

There are a lot of things in life that baffle us—puzzles, riddles, mysteries that we grapple with and cannot get our minds around. The Bible looks many of life's puzzles square in the eye.

In Ecclesiastes, for instance, a sore question is raised and looked at from all sides: does life have any meaning? Is there any real profit to it when all is said and done? Is there enough plus in life to make up for all the minuses of disappointment, frustration and sorrow?

And Job, too, throws the spotlight on questions men and women have grappled with throughout human history. Is righteousness always rewarded in this life? Is suffering always a result of sin? Does God always work according to fixed formulas? Can we always explain what he is doing and why?

It's part of the greatness of the Bible that it airs the problems that bother us. Sometimes we are afraid to, because we feel that God will not accept our doubts. But the Bible itself contains lots of examples of questioning, even arguing with God.

The key is our attitude. If we throw up questions as barriers or hedges to try to keep God at a distance, we are in real trouble. If we use our doubts as shields to protect ourselves from God's demands, our doubts may damn us. But doubts can also be stepping stones to faith.

If God is God, we should expect to be plagued by questions. What kind of God would we have, if we could fully understand everything he said or did? Because he is so great, his word and his ways may baffle us at times. There are wonders and mysteries in his doings that stagger our imagination and tax our minds beyond their capacities. So it's not the presence or absence of questions that makes the difference.

Don't think you are particularly holy if you never find any problems popping into your heart and mind. Some of the great men of Scripture had plenty of questions to deal with. Jeremiah is a good example. He begins one of his prayers with the complaint to God: "O Lord thou hast deceived me" (Jeremiah 20:1).

It's not, then, whether or not we have questions that counts, but what prompts the questions. Are we playing games with God, trying to elude his grasp and fend off his claims? Are we looking for excuses not to believe? Or do we come to him with open heart, yet with sincere problems? Are we willing to accept his answers or even to keep trusting him when we don't yet have an answer?

I suppose it comes down to this: are we willing to let God be God? Are we willing both to bring our questions to him and also to let him tell us whether or not he wants to answer them? He is not a riddle to be solved, a button to be pushed, a toy to be enjoyed or a tool to be manipulated. He is Lord of the universe. He is not at our disposal; we are at his.

The psalmists knew this. They are prime examples of the way devout believers handle honest doubts.

Their psalms are always in season, because they express just the kinds of emotions we all have, not only praise and adoration but uncertainty and bewilderment.

Psalm 49 is a case in point. We call it a wisdom psalm, because it is neither prayer nor praise but instruction. It distills for us the experiences of a wise man in the same way that the Books of Proverbs and Job do. Our wise man has learned some costly lessons, and he is anxious to share them with his hearers.

As a great Old Testament scholar says, every proverb is like locking the stable door after the horse is stolen. What he means is that proverbs are learned only after painful observation. How many people made fools of themselves by rashness before someone coined the saying, "Look before you leap"? Wisdom gained by experience is too precious to be wasted, too valuable not to be shared. So our psalmist in Psalm 49 calls a worldwide audience to listen: "My mouth shall speak wisdom; the meditation of my heart shall be understanding" (v. 3).

The wisdom and understanding that the teacher seeks to share have to do with his attitude toward people who do not put their trust in God and yet seem to succeed. As we read the psalm we gain the impression that he was once vexed over the wealth and prosperity of godless men.

For the wicked to flourish caused problems for many Israelites. They felt that God should always judge evil men and reward righteous ones immediately. When God seemed to ignore wickedness, they did not know what to make of God's silence. And the problem became increasingly troublesome if the rich used their power to afflict or persecute the poor and then seemed to get away with it.

When he first began to tussle with these problems, the psalmist was confused and perplexed. But along the way the issues became clear and he is now able to share his insights.

Two lessons stand out like lighthouses in his experiences and learning—a lesson of folly and a lesson of faith. Strangely enough the psalmist establishes these points by citing **death** as the evidence. The dark mystery of death becomes to him a bright light that clarifies the issues of life.

1. A Lesson of Folly

Death teaches him a lesson of folly—the folly that thinks it can elude the grave. He sees death as a great leveler. It reminds all men of their limitations. It's a hedge against our insolence.

Now what these evil, ambitious men were doing to the psalmist we cannot be sure. There are two main possibilities I suppose. They may have foreclosed on his property and threatened to snatch it from him or they may have been using their wealth to bring false charges against him in court, perhaps by bribing the judge and witnesses.

Whatever the plot or conspiracy is, the writer has learned to take it in stride: "Why should I fear in times of trouble, when the iniquity of my persecutors surrounds me, men who trust in their wealth and boast of the abundance of their riches" (vv. 5, 6).

Their intent may be destructive, and their tactics may be ruthless; but their end is assured. Death is their fate. Twice the psalmist uses these words to drive his point home: "Man cannot abide in his pomp; he is like the beasts that perish" (vv. 12, 20). And along the way he says, "Death shall be their shepherd" (v. 14).

In other words, they are not masters of their own fates, captains of their own souls, no matter what their boasted pomp and show. Death is their master. They may try to lord it over the poor and helpless, but death is their real lord. He has the last word.

We should make clear that the Bible is not against wealth in itself. All our possessions are created by God, who in the beginning called his creation good. Material goods are not by definition sinful. Gold, silver, jewels, houses, lands, herds, automobiles are not necessarily wicked or corrupting.

Yet at the same time wealth carries with it certain hazards, special pitfalls which ought to be recognized. I suppose the greatest inherent danger in wealth is its **deception.** It may mislead those who have it and those who don't.

Surely this is what Christ had in mind when he said that "it is easier for a camel to go through the eye of a needle than for a rich man to enter the kingdom of God" (Matthew 19:24). The apostle Paul echoed this note when he branded "the love of money" as the "root of all evil" (I Timothy 6:10).

Money can give us a false sense of security. It can seduce us into thinking we are more important than we are. It gives us leverage to get our way. It puts others at our beck and call and may even buy us the right to abuse them. So we think anyway. Wealth may deceive us into thinking that we are self-reliant.

Wisdom and fame are equally deceptive, and the psalmist does not miss the mark when he says that "even the wise die, the fool and the stupid alike must perish and leave their wealth to others" (v. 10). False confidence in anything we are or have is deceptive.

That's why the psalmist is so intrigued with death. It is the great demonstration, the unanswerable argument that man is not master of his universe.

Wealth has another hazard that we cannot miss. It not only may deceive those who have it and lure them into oppressive and disdainful ways, but it also deceives those who do not have it. It can spawn envy and covetousness in the hearts of those who press their noses to the windows of the rich and long for what they have. This is undoubtedly why the writer warns his hearers about the foolishness of false trust. He tells them not to fear the wealthy or to envy their riches: "Be not afraid when one becomes rich . . . for when he dies he will carry nothing away" (vv. 16, 17).

You've heard the story about the two men watching the funeral procession of a prominent man in their community. "How much did he leave?" one asked the other. "He left it all," the wise friend replied. And we do, don't we?

How foolish it is for us to allow material gains to lure us into thinking that we are self-sufficient or that goods are more important than people. "Foolish confidence" the psalmist calls this attitude, and what a temptation it is for all of us. Our goods cannot make us fully happy while we have them, and they offer no protection when death calls.

2. A Lesson of Faith

We have more to learn from this psalm than a lesson of folly—the folly of those who think they can elude the grave. There is also a lesson of faith, the psalmist's own faith which reaches out beyond the grave. Sure he knows the reality of death and yet reaches out beyond it to a lasting relationship with God.

Listen to his expression of confidence: "But God

will ransom my soul from the power of Sheol, for he will receive me" (v. 15). Earlier he has said that no amount of wealth can buy ransom from the grave. Here he rejoices in God's ransom.

Sheol, the gloomy abode of the dead that Old Testament believers talked about and feared, is not his final home. His faith in God reaches beyond. True, he gives no details, no clear description. We have to wait for the New Testament and the bright words of Christ to give us that. But our psalmist friend knows that God is greater than death. He senses a relationship with him that death cannot sever.

This relationship with God steadies him in the face of opposition and persecution. Life may seem out of joint with oppression and injustice. But if we know and trust God, we can patiently wait for his justice to be done.

Christ has taught us and shown us that death is not the end. Don't bank on the fleeting, fading aspects of life. Death will dash all hopes that aren't based on God, the immortal King of glory. Trust him and everything else will fall into line.

Psalm 49 is a psalm for all seasons, and especially for times like ours. The Lord may test us by poverty or he may test us by wealth. The key issue is not what we have or don't have, but how we react to our lot in life. Affluence may make us proud and independent. Poverty may make us bitter and covetous. But this is not necessarily and automatically so.

If we accept what we have as gifts of God and do the best we can with what he gives us, we can avoid both arrogance and envy. What really counts for rich, poor, or middle class is whether we truly trust God.

And God, himself, has helped us to do just that by sending his Son. In him death, which has crouched in ambush to catch every man since Adam, is put to death, and life—true life—is made possible.

The psalmist yearned for life beyond the grave. What he hoped for, Christ has promised. And he backed his promise with his resurrection.

Prayer: God, our heavenly Father, by the reality of death you remind us of our limitations and our frailty and by the death and resurrection of your Son you instruct us in your love and power. Thank you, Father, for both lessons. Help us to learn them well. In Jesus' mighty name we pray. Amen.

CHAPTER 13

The Great Return

PSALM 51

God never intended that we keep his grace to ourselves. His grace is his love shared freely with us when
we do not deserve it. Grace hoarded is not grace. The
person who thinks he deserves God's love, who sees
himself as worthy of God's special favor, has missed
the point of grace completely.

Grace is not salary for what we do regularly in
God's behalf. It is not a bonus for efforts above and
beyond the call of duty. Grace is **God's commitment**
to us when we are not able to commit ourselves to
him. It is God's free gift based on his boundless love
and our crying need.

Grace is not only free; it is limitless. God's supply
is not drained by his constant generosity. In the
1930's, during the great depression, John D. Rocke-
feller gave away dimes. He was a multimillionaire, but
his supply of wealth was not inexhaustible so he
parceled it out carefully. His gifts were limited, and
not everyone received. Not so with God. One of my
favorite gospel songs, "He Giveth More Grace," pin-
points this: "His love hath no limit; his grace hath no
measure; his power hath no boundary known unto
men. For out of his infinite riches in Jesus, he giveth,
and giveth, and giveth again."

The psalmists knew this and they never neglected

celebrating God's grace. That's why their psalms are always in season. Think especially of David, who in Psalm 51 openly, honestly, and fervently describes what God's grace means to him.

David, the man after God's own heart. This man, the king, sinned deliberately, extensively, and tragically, committing adultery with Bathsheba and murdering her husband. Apart from God's grace forgiveness was not available. No man could forgive him because his sin had shattered God's law and offended God's love. No sacrifice was acceptable because the entire sacrificial system was designed for unintentional and accidental sin, not for willful sin.

David's prayers acknowledge this terrible reality: "For thou hast no delight in sacrifice; were I to give a burnt offering, thou wouldst not be pleased" (v. 16). And he knows that, because God's law was broken and God's people abused. God himself was sinned against: "Against thee, thee only, have I sinned, and done that which is evil in thy sight" (v. 4).

What could he do but cast himself on the mercy of God, abandon himself totally to the grace of God? Yet because he treasures God's grace so highly, he knows he cannot keep it to himself. Therefore, part of his confession is a vow to tell others. Folded into his plea for forgiveness is his promise to make God's grace manifest to others: "Then I will teach transgressors thy ways, and sinners will return to Thee" (v. 13). Grace is meant to be shared not stored. And hand in hand with David's own return to God is his pledge to call others to make the great return.

1. It Is Sinners Who Return

The word return is used in many connections. Fishermen return to port after a long night at sea.

Children return, shoes muddied from their explorations on a homeward stroll from school. Soldiers return after months of lonely duty overseas. And their return sparks a happy reunion. They've been missed; their place at the table has been empty; but now their fellowship is restored.

The return that David speaks of is so great because it is sinners who are bidden to return, those men whom we would naturally shy away from, whose words are foul, whose acts are repulsive. Ordinarily such men and women are not welcome. They have been kicked out of home and family with shouts of "Get out and never come back!" or "Good riddance for bad rubbish!" Their noses sting from the slap of doors slammed in their faces.

But David, a wounded sinner himself, has experienced the healing grace of God, and pleads with the sinner to return. **Transgressors,** he calls them—mutineers, rebels, renegades who have defied God's authority and pitted their will against his. **Sinners,** he brands them—men who have missed the mark, lives aimed wide of God's target, souls falling short of God's standard.

Yet their rebellion is not permanent; their lost lives are retrievable; their veering course can be altered. Mid-course corrections are possible by turning around and facing the One who made them and loves them. When they do, it's a great return, because God's grace is more than a match for their sin.

2. The Return Brings Bountiful Results

The psalmist is eager to spell out all the benefits of this return. The return is great because its benefits are many.

Cleansing, for instance. "Purge me with hyssop,

and I shall be clean; wash me and I shall be whiter than snow" (v. 7). We can all identify with David's feeling here. Grubbiness leaves us squirming and uncomfortable, like the bits of hair that stick under our collars after visiting the barber. Guilt sticks to us far closer, and leaves us longing to be clean. Return, David says, and find cleansing. Not just of the outside but of the heart itself, the center of our thinking and choosing: "Create in me a clean heart, O God, and put a new and right spirit within me" (v. 10).

Returning means fellowship as well as cleansing. What does righteousness have in common with lawlessness? How can holiness rub shoulders with iniquity? David knows—because he knows who God is—that the persistent, impenitent sinner cannot be on good terms with God. "Cast me not away from thy presence, and take not thy holy Spirit from me" (v. 11). In this desperate petition David acknowledges the great gulf that our sin places between us and God. We cannot stay with him, and he will not stay with us as long as we continue to rebel, casting God's grace aside like some worthless trinket.

Our return is great because it restores us to fellowship with God and his people. The key is in the door. The porch light burns brightly. A welcome fire warms the room. And the God of all grace together with his rescued people cry out, "Come back! All can be well. We love you, whatever you have done."

Cleansing, fellowship, and joy: these are the benefits offered to one who returns. "Fill me with joy and gladness; let the bones which thou hast broken rejoice" (v. 8). And again, "Restore unto me the joy of thy salvation" (v. 12). This great return that David encourages us to make is not a weary trek to some dreary shack. It's a return home with joy. It smacks of celebration. It means dropping our burdens, renewing our purposes, making new friends, and becoming acquainted with God. David's promise flashes with hope: "Then I will teach transgressors thy ways, and sinners will return to thee" (v. 13).

3. It Is to God That We Return

I have only hinted at the best feature of this return. God is the one waiting for us. Because our sin is against him there is no real return except to him.

Return and escape are not the same. When faced with our sin, we are tempted to run away. We may skip from place to place, finding a bit of relief here and a spot of respite there. But there is no solution until we return to God.

The reason for this is that God is the cause of our problem. Obviously, I don't mean that he caused us to sin. What I do mean is that he makes us uncomfortable in our sin. God's continual prodding makes it difficult for us to be complacent. Nudging our consciences, wrestling with our wills, he keeps us on edge about who we are and what we do.

However, God only needles us about our problems to discourage us from trusting false solutions. What he really desires is our return to him. Who else has the full prescription for all that ails us?

How can we describe what it means to return to God? Take all the homecomings and class reunions you've ever attended and roll them into one: you still don't have an inkling. Add to them your Thanksgiving and Christmas gatherings, birthday celebrations and New Year's parties: you still have miles to go. Throw in your honeymoon, your silver wedding anniversary: you have scarcely started.

You are called to return to God. In love and

compassion, in care and concern, in discipline and guidance he is unmatched, unrivaled. His love knows no limits and his grace no measure. His call to us is not to "shape-up or ship-out"; not to "try harder" or "do better"; but to return. There is no finer invitation in life.

Prayer: Heavenly Father, this is a good word because it rings with hope when we had almost given up. It's a welcome word because it tells us that your door is still open. By your grace give us the good sense to turn in our tracks and return, not to the blind alleys of escape but to your loving arms. We pray through Jesus Christ who made this possible. Amen.

Conclusion

"Psalms for All Seasons" is more than a title. It is our assurance that whatever crisis in life we face, we can face with God. He heard the cry of the psalmists centuries ago, and he has promised to hear ours.

The Psalms also remind us how to approach God. There is never a time when a psalm is unfitting. However dismal life may seem, praising God is always in season. "Rejoice in the Lord always; again I will say, Rejoice" (Philippians 4:4).

The Psalms have been used for centuries as a pattern for Christian worship and praise. When one book of the Old Testament is selected to be bound up with the New Testament it is the Book of Psalms. This is wonderful yet strange because the men who uttered these words died centuries before our Savior was born. Yet in the Psalms we find the language which is most fitting to address the God and Father of our Lord Jesus Christ.

Even sections of the New Testament are patterned after the Psalms. The song of Mary, the prophecy of Zachariah, the prayer of Simeon are just a few (Luke 1-2).

As you have read these psalms and studied their meaning I trust you have established a pattern that will stick with you. With these thirteen psalms as a guide, roam through the Psalter. Find psalms that match your mood. Find psalms that change your mood.

As you make the Psalms your own, you will join a great company of men and women who for nearly thirty centuries have grounded their praises and prayers in these ancient words. Kings and peasants, prophets and priests, wisemen and commoners, apostles and martyrs, monks and reformers, housewives and judges—for all of them the Psalms have been spiritual life and breath. Learn from their example.

These chapters are but a sampling. There are one hundred thirty seven yet to go. Enough to last for a goodly season. Enough psalms, in fact, for all seasons.